Mechanic Mike's Machines

Tanks

A+

Smart Apple Media

Published by Smart Apple Media, an imprint of Black Rabbit Books
P.O. Box 3263, Mankato, Minnesota 56002
www.smartapplemedia.com

Produced by David West Children's Books
6 Princeton Court, 55 Felsham Road, London SW15 1AZ

Designed and illustrated by David West

Copyright © 2016 David West Children's Books

Cataloging-in-Publication Data is available from the Library of Congress.
ISBN 978-1-62588-069-7

Printed in China
CPSIA compliance information: DWCB15CP
311214

9 8 7 6 5 4 3 2 1

Mechanic Mike says:
This little guy will tell you something more about the machine.

Find out what type of weapons the tank has.

Discover something you didn't know.

In which wars has the tank seen action?

How many crew or people does it carry?

Get your amazing fact here!

Contents

First Tank

The first tanks were used by the British army in World War I. They had a gun and a machine gun on each side.

Mechanic Mike says:
To keep the first tank secret, the makers said they were building water tanks. The word "tank" has stuck ever since.

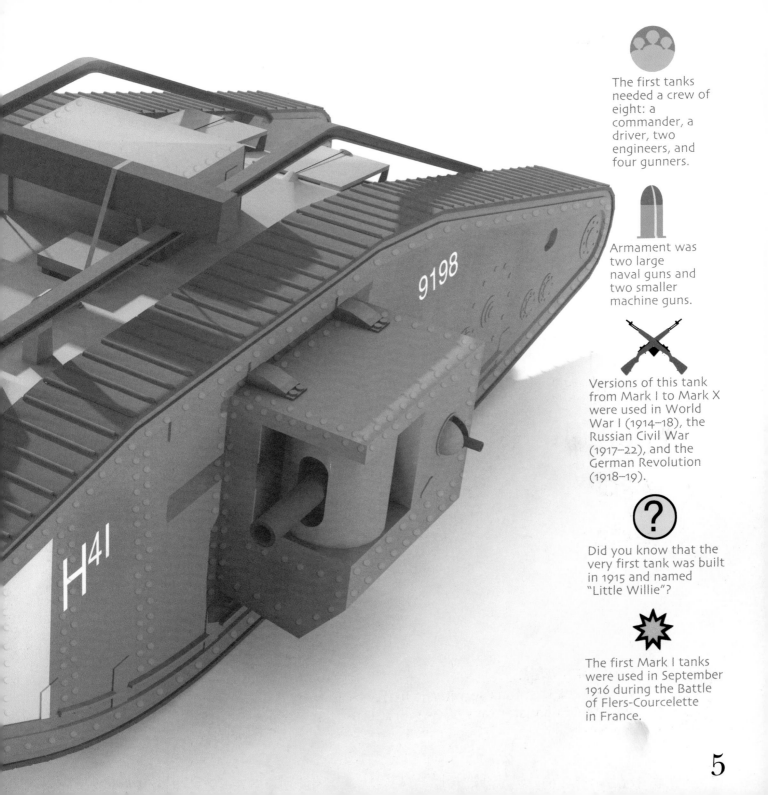

The first tanks needed a crew of eight: a commander, a driver, two engineers, and four gunners.

Armament was two large naval guns and two smaller machine guns.

Versions of this tank from Mark I to Mark X were used in World War I (1914–18), the Russian Civil War (1917–22), and the German Revolution (1918–19).

Did you know that the very first tank was built in 1915 and named "Little Willie"?

The first Mark I tanks were used in September 1916 during the Battle of Flers-Courcelette in France.

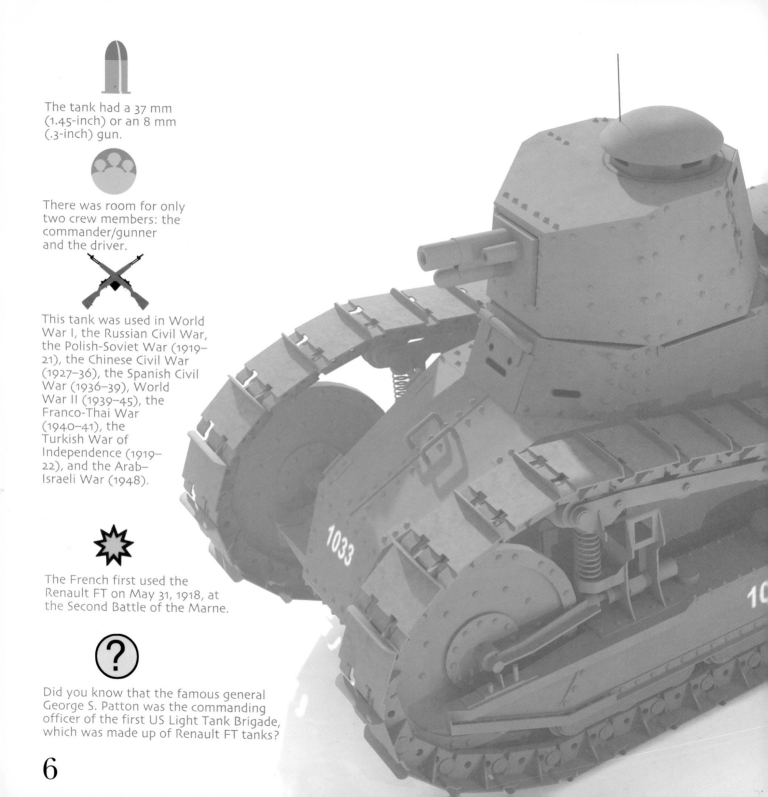

The tank had a 37 mm (1.45-inch) or an 8 mm (.3-inch) gun.

There was room for only two crew members: the commander/gunner and the driver.

This tank was used in World War I, the Russian Civil War, the Polish-Soviet War (1919–21), the Chinese Civil War (1927–36), the Spanish Civil War (1936–39), World War II (1939–45), the Franco-Thai War (1940–41), the Turkish War of Independence (1919–22), and the Arab–Israeli War (1948).

The French first used the Renault FT on May 31, 1918, at the Second Battle of the Marne.

Did you know that the famous general George S. Patton was the commanding officer of the first US Light Tank Brigade, which was made up of Renault FT tanks?

Light Tank

The Renault FT was the first tank to look like a modern-day tank. It had a rotating **turret** and the engine at the rear. This light tank appeared at the end of World War I and was used by French and US troops.

Mechanic Mike says:
Although these light tanks were out of date by the beginning of World War II, they were still in service until shortly after the war ended.

Heavy Battle Tank

One of the most successful tanks of World War II was the Tiger tank. It had very thick armor and a powerful gun. It was so heavy it was designed to cross rivers up to 6.6 feet (two meters) deep rather than cross weak bridges.

The Tiger had one 88 mm (3.46-inch) gun and two machine guns.

The tiger had a crew of five: the commander, gunner, gun loader, driver, and radio operator.

The Tiger tank was used in World War II by the German army.

The Tiger's armor at the front was 120 mm (4.7 inches) thick. Most tank shells could not penetrate it!

Did you know the Tiger was so heavy, 60 tons (54 t), that it could travel just 121 miles (195 km) before refueling?

Floating Tank

Some light tanks like this Russian PT-76 are **amphibious.** They are used by units to check out areas ahead of the main army.

Mechanic Mike says:
The PT-76 can swim up to 6.3 miles per hour (10.2 km/h). It was designed to swim in the sea and to land on beaches to support soldiers attacking from ships and landing craft.

10

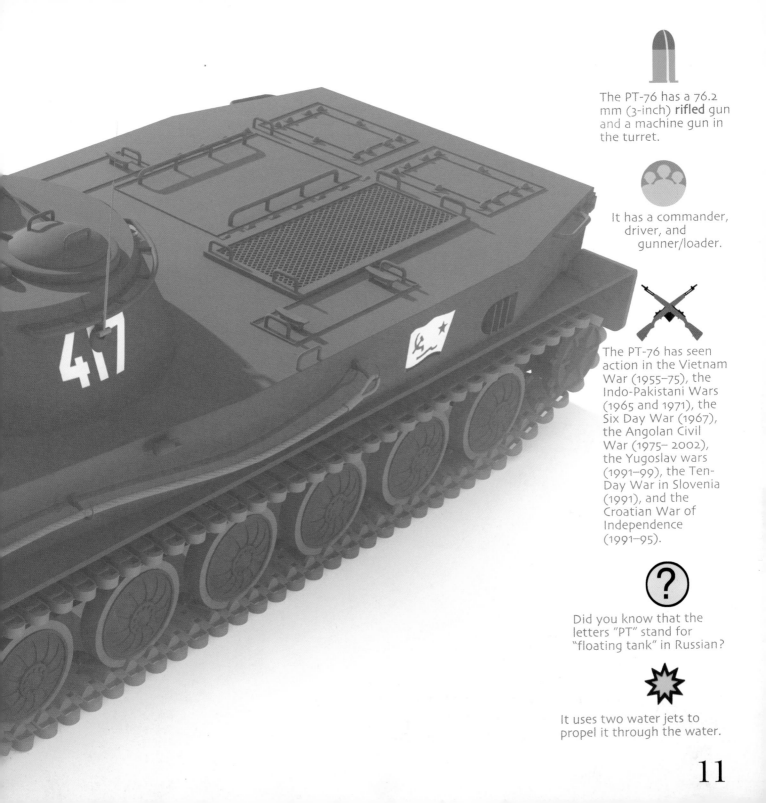

The PT-76 has a 76.2 mm (3-inch) **rifled** gun and a machine gun in the turret.

It has a commander, driver, and gunner/loader.

The PT-76 has seen action in the Vietnam War (1955–75), the Indo-Pakistani Wars (1965 and 1971), the Six Day War (1967), the Angolan Civil War (1975– 2002), the Yugoslav wars (1991–99), the Ten-Day War in Slovenia (1991), and the Croatian War of Independence (1991–95).

Did you know that the letters "PT" stand for "floating tank" in Russian?

It uses two water jets to propel it through the water.

11

MBT (Main Battle Tank)

Main battle tanks like this M1 Abrams are the top tanks of modern armies. They are organized into armored units and supported by soldiers and aircraft.

Mechanic Mike says:
The armor on modern main battle tanks is much lighter than earlier steel armor. It is made of composite and **ceramic** materials and special metals. It can be up to 13 inches (33 cm) thick at the front.

The Abrams has a 105 mm (4.13-inch) rifled cannon or a 120 mm (4.72-inch) smoothbore cannon, one heavy machine gun, and two medium machine guns.

There are four crew: commander, gunner, loader, and driver.

The M1 Abrams was used by the US army in the Gulf War (1990–91), the War in Afghanistan (2001–today), and the Iraq War (2003–11).

Did you know that tanks can fire different kinds of shells? They fire high-explosive anti-tank shells at armored vehicles, and anti-personnel rounds at infantry.

Over 9,000 Abrams tanks have been built. Each costs more than $8 million to make.

IFV

(Infantry Fighting Vehicle)

These small, tank-like vehicles are used to carry soldiers into battle and give fire support. They use weapons like small cannons and missiles that can destroy tanks. This Bradley has a back door for soldiers to get in and out.

The Bradley has a 25 mm (.98-inch) cannon, an anti-tank missile, and one machine gun.

This IFV has three crew: commander, gunner, and driver, as well as six fully equipped soldiers.

Bradleys have been used in the Gulf War and the Iraq War.

During the Gulf War, M2 Bradleys destroyed more Iraqi armored vehicles than the M1 Abrams.

Did you know that the cannon fires up to 200 shells per minute?

14

Mechanic Mike says:
The anti-tank missile is guided to its target by the operator along two thin wires.

Wheeled Tank

Some light tanks, like this B1 Centauro, have wheels instead of tracks. This one can be used as a tank destroyer or as an IFV, which has a smaller turret with a cannon.

Mechanic Mike says:
The B1 Centauro has been used in various countries in Europe for peacekeeping duties. They are usually painted white for these missions.

The Centauro uses the first four wheels to steer.

UN

Like most modern tanks, the Centauro can fire accurately, even when it is moving over rough ground.

Centauros were deployed during the Iraq War.

The B1 Centauro has four crew: commander, gunner, loader, and driver.

The Centauro has a 105 mm (4.13-inch) cannon and two machine guns.

The Churchill AVRE Bridge Layer had the main gun replaced by a **mortar**. This fired a 40-pound (18-kg) explosive-filled projectile nicknamed the Flying Dustbin.

There was a crew of six made up of a driver and five engineers.

The Churchill AVRE Bridge Layer saw action during World War II with the Allied armies (US, Great Britain, and France).

Did you know that the Churchill AVRE was also converted into a plow to dig up enemy mines?

Another bridging machine was the ARK (Armored Ramp Carrier). This was a Churchill tank without a turret that had extendable ramps at each end. Other vehicles could drive up the ramps and over the obstacles.

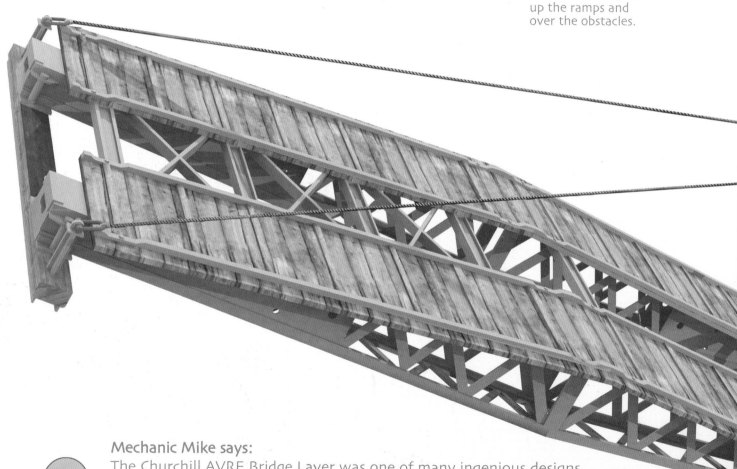

Mechanic Mike says:
The Churchill AVRE Bridge Layer was one of many ingenious designs of World War II known as Hobart's "Funnies." They were forerunners of modern combat-engineering vehicles and were named after the commander Major General Percy Hobart.

18

Bridge Layer

Some tanks have been used to build things in battle. This is a Churchill AVRE Bridge Layer.

Anti-Aircraft

This Russian ZSU-23-4 Shilka is designed to shoot down enemy aircraft. The guns mounted in the turret use **radar** to find the aircraft. They can fire up to 4,000 rounds per minute.

Mechanic Mike says:
Sometimes the barrels of the guns get so hot that the heat sets off the ammunition without the gunner pressing the trigger.

The ZSU-23-4 has four 23 mm (.9-inch) cannons.

It has a crew of four: commander, driver, gunner, and radar operator.

The ZSU has seen action in the Yom Kippur War (1970), the Vietnam War (1955–75), the Lebanese Civil War (1975–90), the Angolan Civil War (1975–2002), the Western Sahara War (1975–91), the Libyan-Egyptian War (1977), the Soviet War in Afghanistan (1979–88), the Iran–Iraq War (1980–88), the Gulf War, the Iraq War, the Libyan Civil War (2011), and the Syrian Civil War (2011 onward).

The guns on the ZSU-23-4 get so hot that each barrel is water-cooled to stop it from overheating.

Did you know that Afghan soldiers nicknamed the ZSU-23-4 the "sewing machine" due to the sound made by the guns firing?

Mobile Artillery

This M109 howitzer is a giant, armored mobile gun. It can fire a shell 11 miles (18 km) or a rocket-assisted projectile (RAP) over 19 miles (30 km).

 The M109 has a 155 mm (6.1-inch) howitzer and one machine gun.

 The M109 has a crew of six: the section chief, the driver, the gunner, the assistant gunner, and two ammunition handlers.

 The M109 has seen action in the Vietnam War, the Yom Kippur War, the Lebanon Wars, the Iran–Iraq War, the Gulf War, and the Iraq War.

 Did you know that the M109 can fire up to six shells in a minute?

 Although this monster weighs 78,000 pounds (35,000 kg), it can out-maneuver a Bradley (see page 14).

Mechanic Mike says:
Howitzers were originally a short-muzzled artillery gun that fired high into the air to drop the shell over enemy defenses. The modern howitzer has a long barrel for better accuracy.

Glossary

amphibious
Suitable for use both on land and in water.

ceramic
A nonmetallic solid that remains hard when it is heated.

mortar
A short gun for firing shells at high angles.

radar
A system for detecting the direction, distance, and speed of an object.

rifled
Having a barrel with spiral grooves inside to make a shell spin for greater accuracy.

turret
The part of a tank that protects the main gun.

Index